Introduction to E-Marketing:

E-marketing, also known as digital marketing or online marketing, is the practice of promoting products or services through the use of electronic media. It encompasses a wide range of activities, including search engine optimization (SEO), social media marketing, email marketing, and online advertising.

One of the key benefits of e-marketing is its ability to reach a global audience. With the internet being readily available around the world, businesses can easily promote their products or services to a wider customer base than traditional marketing methods would allow. Additionally, e-marketing allows for more precise targeting of specific demographics, such as age, location, and interests.

Search engine optimization (SEO) is one of the most important components of e-marketing. It involves optimizing a website to rank higher in search engine results for specific keywords related to the products or services the business offers. This can be achieved through a variety of techniques, such as creating high-quality content, building backlinks, and ensuring the website is mobile-friendly.

Social media marketing is another important aspect of e-marketing. It involves using social media platforms, such as Facebook, Twitter, and Instagram, to promote a business's products or services. This can be done through creating engaging content, running social media ads, and interacting with customers on the platforms.

Email marketing is another key e-marketing strategy. This involves sending promotional emails to a list of subscribers. It can be used to promote new products or services, offer discounts, or provide updates about the business.

Online advertising is also a common e-marketing strategy. This includes using platforms like Google AdWords and Facebook Ads to display ads to a targeted audience.

Overall, e-marketing is a powerful tool for businesses looking to reach a wider audience and promote their products or services. By understanding the basics of e-marketing, businesses can develop effective digital marketing strategies to increase their online presence and drive sales.

Chapter 1 : Setting Up Your Online Presence: Building a Website and Creating Social Media Profiles

Setting up an online presence is crucial for any business looking to establish a presence on the internet. This can be achieved by building a website and creating social media profiles.

Building a website is the first step in creating an online presence. A website is the foundation of an online presence and it serves as the primary destination for customers to learn about your business, products, and services. It should be well-designed, easy to navigate and should provide relevant information about your business. The website should be responsive design, which means it should be able to adjust to different screen sizes and devices. This is important because more and more people are accessing the internet through mobile devices.

When building a website, it is important to choose a domain name that is easy to remember and relevant to your business. Additionally, the website should be hosted on a reliable server to ensure it is always available to customers.

Creating social media profiles is another important step in setting up an online presence. Social media platforms, such as Facebook, Twitter, and Instagram, are powerful tools for connecting with customers and promoting your business. By creating profiles on these platforms, businesses can engage with customers, share content, and promote their products or services.

When creating social media profiles, it is important to choose a username that is consistent with your business name and to provide accurate and complete information about your business. Additionally, it is important to keep the profiles active by regularly posting updates and engaging with customers.

Overall, building a website and creating social media profiles are essential steps in setting up an online presence. A well-designed website and active social media profiles can help businesses establish a strong online presence, connect with customers, and promote their products or services.

Another important aspect of setting up an online presence is search engine optimization (SEO). SEO is the process of optimizing a website to rank higher in search engine results for specific keywords related to the products or services the business offers. This is important because when a website ranks higher in search engine results, it is more likely to be seen by potential customers.

To improve a website's SEO, businesses can focus on creating high-quality, relevant content, optimizing the website's structure, and building backlinks from other websites. Additionally, businesses can focus on making the website mobile-friendly, which is becoming increasingly important as more people access the internet through mobile devices.

Another important factor in setting up an online presence is creating a consistent brand image across all platforms. This includes using the same logo, color scheme, and messaging across the website and social media profiles. This helps to create a cohesive image and makes it easier for customers to recognize and remember the brand.

Another important aspect of setting up an online presence is to consider creating a blog or news section in your website. Blogging allows you to connect with your audience by providing valuable information, insights, and updates about your business. By consistently providing valuable content, you can build trust and establish yourself as an authority in your industry.

Lastly, to set up an online presence, it is important to get involved in online communities and forums related to your industry. This can be done by joining groups on social media, participating in online discussions, and providing helpful responses to customer questions. This will help you build relationships with potential customers and increase visibility for your business.

In summary, setting up an online presence is a crucial step for any business looking to establish a presence on the internet. Building a website and creating social media profiles, focusing on SEO, creating a consistent brand image, having a blog, and getting involved in online communities are all important steps in establishing an effective online presence.

Chapter 2: Developing a Target Audience: Identifying and Understanding Your Ideal Customer

Developing a target audience is an essential step in creating effective marketing campaigns and developing a successful business strategy. Identifying and understanding your ideal customer, also known as your target audience, allows you to tailor your products, services, and messaging to meet their specific needs and preferences.

The first step in developing a target audience is to identify the demographics of your ideal customer. This includes information such as age, gender, income, education level, and geographic location. You should also consider psychographics, such as lifestyle, values, and interests. By understanding the demographics and psychographics of your target audience, you can create a clear picture of who your ideal customer is and what they are looking for.

Once you have a general idea of your target audience, you can begin to research and gather more specific information about them. This can include conducting surveys, focus groups, and interviews with current and potential customers. You can also analyze data from your website, social media, and other online platforms to gain insights into your audience's behavior and preferences.

Once you have a solid understanding of your target audience, you can use this information to create targeted marketing campaigns and product development strategies. By tailoring your messaging, products, and services to meet the specific needs and preferences of your target audience, you increase the chances of attracting and retaining customers.

It's important to note that as time goes on, your target audience may change, so it's important to regularly review and update your target audience profile. Additionally, it's also important to be aware of the market trends, consumer behavior and your competitors, which can also impact your target audience.

Overall, developing a target audience is a crucial step in the process of building a successful business. By identifying and understanding your ideal customer, you can create more effective marketing campaigns, develop products and services that meet their needs, and ultimately increase customer satisfaction and loyalty.

Here are the steps to take when developing a target audience:

1. **Define your product or service:** Before you can identify your target audience, you need to have a clear understanding of what you're selling. This includes the features, benefits, and unique selling points of your product or service.

2. **Identify your current customer base:** Look at your current customer base to see if there are any patterns or trends. This can include demographics such as age, gender, income level, and location, as well as psychographics such as interests and values.

3. **Conduct market research:** Conduct surveys, focus groups, and interviews to gather more information about your target audience. This can include their needs, wants, and pain points, as well as their purchasing habits and decision-making processes.

4. **Create buyer personas:** Once you have a good understanding of your target audience, create a buyer persona that represents your ideal customer. This should include information such as demographics, psychographics, pain points, and goals.

5. **Test and refine:** Use your buyer personas to create marketing campaigns and test them with your target audience. Collect feedback and make adjustments as necessary to refine your strategy.

By identifying and understanding your ideal customer, you can create a marketing strategy that is tailored to their needs and interests. This will help you reach the right people and increase the chances of success for your business.

Chapter 3: Creating a Content Strategy: Developing and Promoting Valuable Content

Creating a content strategy is essential for promoting your business and reaching your target audience. Developing and promoting valuable content can help you establish your brand, build trust with your audience, and drive traffic to your website. Here are the steps to take when creating a content strategy:

1. **Define your goals:** Before you start creating content, it's important to have a clear understanding of what you want to achieve. This might include increasing brand awareness, driving website traffic, or generating leads.
2. **Identify your target audience:** Understand who your audience is, what they're interested in, and what their pain points are. This will help you create content that resonates with them and addresses their needs.
3. **Conduct a content audit:** Review your existing content to see what's working and what's not. This will help you identify gaps in your content and make sure that you're not duplicating effort.
4. **Develop a content calendar:** Create a schedule for publishing content, including a mix of different types of content such as blog posts, infographics, videos, and social media updates.
5. **Create valuable content:** Develop high-quality, informative and useful content that will be of interest to your target audience. Use keywords that are relevant to your audience, and optimize your content for search engines.
6. **Promote your content:** Share your content on your website, social media channels, and other platforms where your target audience is active. Use paid promotion to reach a wider audience and increase visibility.
7. **Measure and analyze:** Use analytics tools to track the performance of your content, and use the data to optimize your strategy and improve your future content.

Creating a content strategy helps you focus on creating valuable and relevant content that resonates with your target audience. By developing and promoting high-quality content, you can establish your brand as an authority in your industry and drive more traffic to your website.

In addition to the steps outlined above, here are a few more things to consider when developing your content strategy:

- **Repurposing content:** Not all content needs to be created from scratch. Consider repurposing existing content by updating it, turning it into a video or podcast, or creating a new version for a different audience.
- **Creating a content calendar:** A content calendar can help you stay organized and ensure that you're consistently creating and publishing new content. It also allows you to plan ahead for events, holidays, or other important dates that may impact your content.
- **Collaborating with other teams:** Your content strategy should be a collaboration between your marketing team and other teams within your organization. For example, your product team may have valuable insights into the pain points of your customers, or your customer service team may be able to provide feedback on what types of content are helpful for addressing common customer questions.
- **Utilizing analytics:** Use tools such as Google Analytics, social media analytics, and other metrics to track the performance of your content. This will help you understand which pieces of content are resonating with your audience and which ones aren't.
- **Being consistent:** Consistency is key when it comes to content marketing. You need to be consistent in terms of the quality of your content and the frequency of your posting. This helps you build trust and credibility with your audience.
- **Adapting to changes:** The digital world is constantly evolving, and your content strategy should adapt to these changes. For example, if you notice that your audience is increasingly consuming video content, you may want to shift your focus to creating more videos.

A well-crafted content strategy will help you create content that resonates with your target audience, drives engagement and supports your business objectives. It takes time, effort, and a willingness to adapt and learn from your audience's behavior. It's an ongoing process, but with a clear plan and the right tools, you can create a successful content strategy that helps your business grow.

Chapter 4 : Search Engine Optimization (SEO): Maximizing Your Online Visibility

Search Engine Optimization (SEO) is the process of optimizing a website to improve its visibility in search engine results pages (SERPs). The goal of SEO is to increase the quantity and quality of website traffic by making it easier for people to find your site when they search for relevant keywords.

There are several key elements to SEO, including:

- **On-page optimization:** This includes optimizing the content and structure of your website to make it more search engine friendly. This includes things like using relevant keywords in your content, optimizing your meta tags, and making sure your site is mobile-friendly.
- **Off-page optimization:** This includes building links to your site from other websites, which can help improve your site's visibility in search engine results.
- **Technical SEO:** This includes optimizing the technical elements of your website, such as ensuring your site is properly indexed, making sure it loads quickly, and ensuring it is accessible to both search engines and users.
- **Content strategy:** Creating quality and relevant content is important for SEO. It helps you to target the right audience, increase the dwell time on your site, and also enhances the chances of backlinks.

Here are a few specific actions you can take to improve your SEO:

- **Research keywords:** Identify the keywords and phrases that your target audience is searching for, and make sure they are included throughout your website and in your meta tags.
- **Build high-quality links:** Reach out to other websites and ask them to link to your site. The more high-quality links you have pointing to your site, the higher it will rank in search engine results.
- **Optimize your images and videos:** Use descriptive file names and alt tags for images and videos on your site, as this will help search engines understand the content of these media files.

- **Monitor your progress:** Use tools such as Google Analytics and Google Search Console to track your website's performance in search engine results and monitor your progress over time.
- **Stay up-to-date:** SEO is an ever-changing field, so it's important to stay up-to-date with the latest best practices and algorithm updates.

It's worth noting that SEO is a long-term strategy and it takes time to see the results. There's no magic formula for instantly climbing the search rankings. However, by following best practices, creating quality content, and staying on top of changes to search engine algorithms, you can improve your site's visibility in search engine results and drive more traffic to your site.

- **Local SEO:** If your business has a physical location, it's important to optimize for local search. This includes claiming your Google My Business listing and making sure your business information (such as your address and phone number) is consistent across all online directories.
- **Site architecture:** A well-structured website makes it easy for both search engines and users to navigate. Use a clear hierarchy, including headings and subheadings, and make sure your site's URLs are clean and easy to read.
- **Content Marketing:** Create valuable, informative content that will attract links and social shares. This will help your site to earn backlinks, which is one of the most important ranking factors for SEO.
- **Social media:** Integrate social media with your website. Share your content on social media platforms, engage with your audience, and encourage them to share your content. This can help drive traffic to your site and improve your search rankings.
- **Mobile optimization:** With the increasing use of mobile devices, it's essential to ensure that your site is mobile-friendly and loads quickly on mobile devices.
- **User experience:** User experience is an important factor in SEO. Make sure your site is easy to navigate, loads quickly and has a clean, modern design.
- **Schema markup:** Schema markup is a form of structured data that helps search engines understand the content of your website. It can be used to mark up various types of content, such as reviews, events, and products.

- **Sitemap and Robots.txt:** A sitemap is a file that lists all the pages on your website, and a robots.txt file is used to control which pages search engines can crawl. Both of these files help search engines to understand your site's structure and content.
- **Speed optimization:** Make sure your site loads quickly. A slow-loading site can lead to a high bounce rate, which will negatively impact your search rankings.
- **Monitor your backlinks:** Keep an eye on the backlinks to your site. If you notice any low-quality or spammy links, use the "disavow" tool in Google Search Console to tell Google to ignore those links.

SEO is not a one-time process, it's an ongoing effort. By regularly monitoring your site's performance, staying up-to-date with the latest best practices, and making adjustments as needed, you can continue to improve your search rankings and drive more traffic to your site.

Chapter 5 : Pay-Per-Click Advertising (PPC): Utilizing Online Advertising to Drive Traffic

Pay-Per-Click (PPC) advertising is an online advertising model where advertisers pay each time a user clicks on one of their ads. PPC is a way to quickly drive targeted traffic to a website, and it can be an effective way to generate leads and sales.

One of the most popular platforms for PPC advertising is Google Ads, which is a platform for running ads on Google's search engine and other websites across the web. Other platforms include Bing Ads, which allows you to run ads on Bing and Yahoo search engines, and social media platforms such as Facebook and Instagram.

Here are the key steps to setting up a PPC campaign:

1. **Define your target audience:** Determine who your target audience is and what their interests are. This will help you to create ads that are relevant and appealing to them.
2. **Research keywords:** Identify the keywords that your target audience is searching for and use them to create ad groups.
3. **Create ad copy and visuals:** Create compelling ad copy and visuals that will grab the attention of your target audience. Make sure your ads are clear and concise, and include a call-to-action (CTA) to encourage users to click through to your website.
4. **Set a budget:** Decide how much you are willing to spend on your PPC campaign. Be aware that PPC advertising can be costly, so it's important to set a realistic budget that you can stick to.
5. <u>**Track your results:**</u> Use tools such as Google Analytics to track the performance of your ads, including the number of clicks, conversions, and overall ROI.
6. **Optimize your campaign:** Based on the results of your campaign, make adjustments to improve your results. This may include changing your ad copy, targeting different keywords, or adjusting your budget.

PPC advertising has several advantages over traditional advertising methods. It allows you to reach a targeted audience, track your results in real-time, and make adjustments to your campaign as needed. PPC campaigns can also be set up and launched relatively quickly, which makes it an ideal solution for short-term promotions or for testing new products or services.

However, PPC advertising can be costly, and it's important to keep in mind that you will need to continue to pay for each click, even if the user doesn't convert into a sale or lead. Additionally, PPC advertising can be highly competitive, so it's important to stay up-to-date with the latest best practices and trends in the industry.

Overall, PPC advertising can be a valuable tool for driving targeted traffic to your website and generating leads and sales. By researching your target audience, creating effective ad copy and visuals, and tracking your results, you can optimize your PPC campaign and achieve success.

Another important aspect of PPC advertising is ad placement. Where your ads are placed can greatly impact their performance. Google Ads and Bing Ads allow you to place ads on their search engine results pages (SERPs) as well as on other websites through their display network. Social media platforms like Facebook and Instagram allow you to place ads in the news feed, stories, and other specific locations within the platform.

When it comes to ad placement, it's important to consider the context and relevance of where your ads will appear. For example, ads placed on the SERPs will be more relevant to users who are actively searching for the products or services you offer, whereas ads placed on a website or social media platform may be more effective at reaching users who are in a browsing or discovery mindset.

Another aspect of PPC advertising is ad targeting. Ad targeting refers to the process of reaching a specific audience with your ads. It can be done based on demographics, location, interests, behavior and many other factors. Ad targeting can help you to reach the right audience at the right time and place, which can help to improve the performance of your ads.

Ad extensions are another feature of PPC advertising that can help to improve performance. Ad extensions are additional information that can be added to your ads, such as a phone number, address, or links to specific pages on your website. Ad extensions can help to increase the visibility of your ads and make it more likely that users will click through to your website.

To sum up, PPC advertising can be an effective way to drive targeted traffic to your website and generate leads and sales. By researching your target audience, creating effective ad copy and visuals, tracking your results, and optimizing your campaign, you can achieve success with PPC advertising. Additionally, ad placement, targeting and extensions can greatly impact your campaign performance. However, it is important to keep in mind that PPC advertising can be costly, and it's important to stay up-to-date with the latest best practices and trends in the industry.

Chapter 6: Email Marketing: Building Relationships and Driving Sales

Email marketing is a form of direct digital marketing that uses email as the primary means of communication with a target audience. It is used to build relationships with potential and existing customers and to drive sales.

Here are the key steps to creating an effective email marketing campaign:

1. **Build a list:** To start an email marketing campaign, you will first need to build a list of email addresses of potential and existing customers. You can do this by offering a newsletter sign-up on your website, or by gathering email addresses at events or through other means.
2. **Segment your list:** Once you have a list of email addresses, you can segment it into different groups based on factors such as demographics, purchase history, and interests. This will help you to create targeted, personalized campaigns for different groups of subscribers.
3. **Create engaging content:** The next step is to create engaging content that will appeal to your target audience. This can include text, images, videos, and other types of content. The content should be relevant to the interests of your target audience and should include a clear call-to-action (CTA) that encourages subscribers to take a specific action, such as making a purchase or visiting your website.
4. **Design and send your email:** Design your email using a template or email marketing software and send it out to your list.
5. **Track and analyze the results:** Use tools such as Google Analytics to track the performance of your email campaigns, including the number of opens, clicks, and conversions. Use this data to analyze the results of your campaigns and make adjustments to improve performance.
6. **Optimize your campaign:** Based on the results of your campaign, make adjustments to improve your results. This may include changing your subject lines, adding new segments, or redesigning your email.

Email marketing has several advantages over other forms of digital marketing. It allows you to reach a targeted audience, track your results in real-time, and make adjustments to your campaign as needed. Additionally, it can be highly personalized and can be used to build relationships with potential and existing customers.

However, it's important to keep in mind that email marketing can be time-consuming and costly, and it's important to stay up-to-date with the latest best practices and trends in the industry. Additionally, it's important to comply with laws such as the General Data Protection Regulation (GDPR) and the Canadian Anti-Spam Law (CASL) which regulate email marketing activities.

Overall, email marketing can be a valuable tool for building relationships with potential and existing customers and driving sales. By building a list of email addresses, segmenting your list, creating engaging content, and tracking and analyzing the results of your campaigns, you can optimize your email marketing campaign and achieve success.

Another important aspect of email marketing is the use of automation. Email marketing automation allows you to set up automated email campaigns that are triggered by specific actions or events. For example, you can set up an automated welcome email that is sent to new subscribers, or a series of automated emails that are sent to customers who have abandoned their shopping cart. Automated emails can save time and effort, and can help to improve the performance of your email campaigns.

Another important aspect of email marketing is testing and optimization. A/B testing, also known as split testing, is a method of comparing two versions of an email to see which performs better. This can help you to optimize your emails and improve their performance. Testing can be done on various elements of the email, such as subject line, sending time, personalization, and call-to-action.

Additionally, it's important to consider the mobile experience when it comes to email marketing. More and more people are accessing their emails on mobile devices, so it's important to make sure your emails are mobile-friendly and easy to read on small screens. This means using a responsive design, keeping the content short and simple, and including large, easy-to-tap buttons for calls-to-action.

In conclusion, Email marketing is a powerful tool for building relationships with potential and existing customers and driving sales. By building a list of email addresses, segmenting your list, creating engaging content, and tracking and analyzing the results of your campaigns, you can optimize your email marketing campaign and achieve success. Additionally, automation, testing and optimization can greatly impact your campaign performance. It's important to keep in mind that email marketing can be time-consuming and costly, and it's important to stay up-to-date with the latest best practices and trends in the industry and comply with laws and regulations.

Chapter 7 : Social Media Marketing: Building a Community and Promoting Your Brand

Social media marketing is the process of using social media platforms to promote a product, service, or brand, and to build a community of engaged followers.

It is a cost-effective way to reach a large and targeted audience, and to build relationships with potential and existing customers.

Here are the key steps to creating an effective social media marketing campaign:

1. **Identify your target audience:** The first step in creating a social media marketing campaign is to identify your target audience. This will help you to create content that is relevant to their interests and needs, and to choose the right social media platforms to reach them.
2. **Choose the right platforms:** Once you have identified your target audience, you can choose the social media platforms that are most likely to reach them. Some of the most popular platforms include Facebook, Instagram, Twitter, LinkedIn, and YouTube, but there are many others to consider as well.
3. **Create a content strategy:** Develop a content strategy that aligns with your overall marketing goals. This can include a mix of different types of content such as videos, images, infographics, and blog posts. The key is to create content that is engaging, informative, and relevant to your target audience.
4. **Build a community:** Building a community of engaged followers is an essential part of social media marketing. This can be done by creating and sharing content that inspires conversation and engagement, and by responding to comments and messages in a timely and professional manner.
5. **Use paid advertising:** Social media platforms offer paid advertising options that can help you to reach a larger audience. This includes options such as sponsored posts, promoted accounts, and paid influencer campaigns.
6. **Analyze and optimize:** Use social media analytics tools to track the performance of your campaigns, including the number of likes, shares,

comments, and conversions. Use this data to analyze the results of your campaigns and make adjustments to improve performance.

Social media marketing has several advantages over other forms of digital marketing. It allows you to reach a large and targeted audience, to build relationships with potential and existing customers, and to track your results in real-time. Additionally, social media platforms are constantly evolving, so it's important to stay up-to-date with the latest best practices and trends in the industry.

However, it's important to keep in mind that social media marketing can be time-consuming and costly, and it's important to have a clear strategy in place. Additionally, it's important to comply with the terms of service and community guidelines of each platform.

Overall, social media marketing is an effective way to promote a product, service, or brand and to build a community of engaged followers. By identifying your target audience, choosing the right platforms, creating a content strategy, building a community, using paid advertising, and analyzing and optimizing your campaigns, you can achieve success with your social media marketing efforts.

Another key aspect of social media marketing is engaging with your audience. Engagement is essential in building and maintaining a strong relationship with your followers. This can be done by encouraging conversation, asking questions, and responding to comments and messages in a timely manner. Additionally, social media platforms offer features such as polls, quizzes, and live streaming, which can be used to increase engagement and create a more interactive experience for your followers.

Another key aspect of social media marketing is influencer marketing. Influencer marketing involves partnering with individuals who have a large following on social media, in order to reach a larger audience. Influencers can be used to promote your product or service, or to create sponsored content. It's important to choose influencers who align with your brand and target audience.

Additionally, it's important to track your progress and measure the success of your social media marketing efforts. There are several social media analytics tools available that can help you to track metrics such as the number of followers, likes, shares, comments, and conversions. By monitoring these metrics, you can see which tactics are working and which aren't, and make adjustments as necessary.

Another important aspect of social media marketing is compliance with laws and regulations, such as the Federal Trade Commission's (FTC) guidelines for sponsored content and endorsements. It's important to disclose any sponsored content or partnerships, and to ensure that all claims made in your social media marketing are truthful and not misleading.

In conclusion, social media marketing is a powerful way to promote a product, service, or brand and to build a community of engaged followers. By identifying your target audience, choosing the right platforms, creating a content strategy, engaging with your audience, using influencer marketing, tracking your progress, and staying compliant with laws and regulations, you can achieve success with your social media marketing efforts. It's important to keep in mind that social media marketing can be time-consuming and costly, and to always be aware of the latest best practices and trends in the industry.

Chapter 8 : Analytics and Measurement: Tracking and Analyzing Your E-Marketing Efforts

Analytics and measurement are essential for tracking and analyzing the effectiveness of your e-marketing efforts. By collecting and analyzing data on your website, email campaigns, social media, and other digital channels, you can gain valuable insights into your audience, your marketing campaigns, and your overall performance.

One of the key tools for analytics and measurement is web analytics. Web analytics software, such as Google Analytics, can be used to track and analyze data on your website, such as the number of visitors, their behavior, and the sources of their traffic. By analyzing this data, you can gain insights into which pages on your website are the most popular, which sources are driving the most traffic, and which pages are most likely to convert visitors into customers.

Another important aspect of analytics and measurement is email marketing analytics. Email marketing software, such as Mailchimp or Constant Contact, includes built-in analytics that allow you to track and analyze the performance of your email campaigns. Metrics such as open rates, click-through rates, and conversion rates can be used to measure the success of your email campaigns and to identify areas for improvement.

Social media analytics is another important aspect of analytics and measurement. Social media platforms, such as Facebook, Twitter, and Instagram, provide their own analytics tools that allow you to track metrics such as likes, shares, comments, and followers. Additionally, you can use third-party tools, such as Hootsuite or Sprout Social, to gain a more comprehensive view of your social media performance.

In addition to the specific e-marketing channels, it's important to have a holistic view of your e-marketing efforts. Cross-channel analytics platforms like Omniture, Adobe Analytics and Google Analytics 360 can give you an overview of how all your channels are performing together, and how they're impacting each other. This will help you to identify the most effective channels and campaigns, and to make data-driven decisions about your e-marketing strategy.

Another important aspect of analytics and measurement is A/B testing. A/B testing involves creating two versions of a campaign, and then sending one version to a control group and the other version to a test group. By comparing the performance of the two groups, you can identify which version of the campaign is more effective. This can be done for various elements of a campaign such as subject lines, calls to action, images, and content.

Another important aspect of analytics and measurement is setting clear goals and objectives. Before launching any marketing campaign, it's essential to have a clear understanding of what you want to achieve. This could be anything from increasing website traffic to boosting sales, building brand awareness, or growing your social media following. Setting clear goals and objectives will help you to measure the success of your campaigns and to identify areas for improvement.

Once you have set your goals and objectives, you can use key performance indicators (KPIs) to track your progress. KPIs are specific metrics that you can use to measure the performance of your campaigns and to determine whether or not you are achieving your goals. Some examples of KPIs for website analytics include: bounce rate, pages per session, and time on site. For email marketing, open rates, click-through rates, and conversion rates are important. For social media, engagement rate, reach, and follower growth are key indicators.

It's also important to regularly analyze and interpret your data. The insights you gain from your analytics can help you to optimize your e-marketing efforts and to make data-driven decisions. For example, if your website analytics show that most of your traffic is coming from a particular source, you may want to focus more on that channel and invest more resources in it.

If your email campaigns have a high open rate but a low click-through rate, you may want to focus on creating more compelling subject lines and calls to action.

Additionally, it's important to consider the context in which your data is collected. For example, if you see a sharp drop in website traffic, it could be the result of a technical issue or a change in your target audience.

Understanding the context of the data will help you to make more accurate conclusions.

In conclusion, analytics and measurement are essential for tracking and analyzing the effectiveness of your e-marketing efforts. By using web analytics, email marketing analytics, social media analytics, and cross-channel analytics, you can gain valuable insights into your audience, your marketing campaigns, and your overall performance. Additionally, A/B testing can be used to identify the most effective elements of a campaign. With the right tools and approach, you can improve the performance of your e-marketing efforts and achieve better results.

Conclusion : Putting it All Together and Achieving E-Marketing Success

In conclusion, e-marketing is a complex and ever-evolving field that requires a strategic and holistic approach. To achieve e-marketing success, it's essential to start by developing a clear and comprehensive e-marketing strategy that takes into account all the different elements of e-marketing, including content strategy, SEO, PPC, email marketing, social media marketing, and analytics and measurement.

Creating a content strategy is an essential part of e-marketing. Developing and promoting valuable content will help you to attract and engage your target audience, establish your brand as an authority in your industry, and drive traffic to your website. To maximize your online visibility, it's important to invest in SEO, which involves optimizing your website and content for search engines.

PPC advertising can be an effective way to drive traffic and increase brand awareness. By utilizing online advertising platforms such as Google Ads, you can reach a targeted audience and achieve measurable results. Email marketing is also an effective e-marketing tool that can help you to build relationships with your audience and drive sales.

Social media marketing is an essential part of e-marketing that can help you to build a community and promote your brand. By engaging with your audience on social media platforms, you can increase brand awareness, build relationships, and drive traffic to your website.

Finally, analytics and measurement are an essential part of e-marketing. By tracking and analyzing your e-marketing efforts, you can identify areas for improvement and make data-driven decisions to optimize your campaigns and achieve e-marketing success.

E-marketing is a continuous process, and you will have to keep on experimenting, learning, and adapting to the changes in the field. With a strategic and holistic approach, you can develop an effective e-marketing strategy that helps you to achieve your business goals and drive measurable results.

In summary, achieving e-marketing success requires a strategic and holistic approach that includes understanding your target audience, consistency, measurement and analysis, budgeting and staying up-to-date with the latest trends and developments in e-marketing.

Table des matières